Put Beginning Readers on the Right Track with
ALL ABOARD READING™

The All Aboard Reading series is especially for beginning readers. Written by noted authors and illustrated in full color, these are books that children really and truly *want* to read—books to excite their imagination, tickle their funny bone, expand their interests, and support their feelings. With four different reading levels, All Aboard Reading lets you choose which books are most appropriate for your children and their growing abilities.

Picture Readers—for Ages 3 to 6
Picture Readers have super-simple texts, with many nouns appearing as rebus pictures. At the end of each book are 24 flash cards—on one side is the rebus picture; on the other side is the written-out word.

Level 1—for Preschool through First-Grade Children
Level 1 books have very few lines per page, very large type, easy words, lots of repetition, and pictures with visual "cues" to help children figure out the words on the page.

Level 2—for First-Grade to Third-Grade Children
Level 2 books are printed in slightly smaller type than Level 1 books. The stories are more complex, but there is still lots of repetition in the text, and many pictures. The sentences are quite simple and are broken up into short lines to make reading easier.

Level 3—for Second-Grade through Third-Grade Children
Level 3 books have considerably longer texts, harder words, and more complicated sentences.

All Aboard for happy reading!

For James and the frog
in Rittenhouse Square—L.D.

For my nature-loving friend, Corey—J.M.

Cut-paper photography by Paul Dyer.

Special thanks to John Behler, Curator, Department of Herpetology,
Wildlife Conservation Society, Bronx, NY.

Text copyright © 1998 by Laura Driscoll. Illustrations copyright © 1998 by Judith Moffatt.
All rights reserved. Published by Grosset & Dunlap, Inc., a member of Penguin Putnam Books
for Young Readers, New York. ALL ABOARD READING is a trademark of The Putnam &
Grosset Group. GROSSET & DUNLAP is a trademark of Grosset & Dunlap, Inc. Published
simultaneously in Canada. Printed in the U.S.A.

Library of Congress Cataloging-in-Publication Data

Driscoll, Laura.
  Frogs / by Laura Driscoll ; illustrated by Judith Moffatt.
    p.   cm.—(All aboard reading. Level 1)
  Summary : An introduction to amphibians as tiny as a fingertip or as large as a foot whose
tails little by little shrink and disappear.
  1. Frogs—Juvenile literature. [1. Frogs.] I. Moffatt, Judith, ill. II. Title. III. Series.
QL668.C2D75   1998
597.8'9—dc21
97-43359
CIP
AC

ISBN 0-448-41868-1 (GB) A B C D E F G H I J
ISBN 0-448-41839-8 (pbk.) A B C D E F G H I J

ALL
ABOARD
READING™

Level 1
Preschool-Grade 1

FROGS

By Laura Driscoll
Illustrated by Judith Moffatt

Grosset & Dunlap • New York

Ker-plunk!

Something splashes
into the pond.

A frog!

It has strong back legs.

It has webbed feet.

It swims fast.

Frogs feel at home
in the pond.
Why?
Because they begin life
in the water—
as tiny frog eggs.
In the spring,
a mother frog
lays lots of eggs.

The eggs hatch.
Frog babies swim out.
They look like fish.
They swim like fish.
They even breathe
underwater like fish.

But they are not fish.

They are tadpoles.

They will grow up to be frogs.

Soon the tadpoles change.
They get bigger.
They grow little back legs,
then front legs.

And little by little,
their tails shrink
and disappear!

Something also changes
inside them.
Now the baby frogs
can breathe out of the water,
like we do.

The frogs hop onto a log.
They are now land animals.
They still can swim.
But they are not
water animals anymore.

frog

Animals that change this way
are called <u>amphibians</u>.
(You say it like this:
am-FIH-bee-uns.)
Are frogs the only amphibians?

toad

No!

Toads are amphibians, too.

Toads usually have
bumpy skin and shorter legs
than frogs.

There are about 4,000
kinds of frogs.
They live all over the world.
Most frogs are
the size of your hand.

But the biggest frog
is called the Goliath frog,
like the giant.

This picture is about
the same size as the real frog.

Tree frogs are so tiny
they can stand
on your fingertip.
Can you guess
where tree frogs live?
In trees!
Their sticky toes
help them hold on tight!

Sometimes at night
you can hear tree frogs croak.
Lots of frogs croak.
They croak to find mates.

They also croak
to warn other frogs
of danger.
Many animals
like to eat frogs.

But these pretty frogs are safe.
Why doesn't the bird eat them?
Because they have poison
on their skin.

Snakes like to eat frogs.
But this Asian leaf frog is safe.
The snake cannot see it
in the pile of leaves.
The frog stays very still.
Soon the snake goes away.

The barking frog

fools its enemies another way.

It puffs itself up.

Now it looks too big to eat.

But most frogs in danger
do the same thing.
They hop away—fast!

Ker-plunk!